Abound
with Blessings

D1601155

Abound with Blessings

A Month of Poems and Prayers

Julia H. Crim and Keith R. Crim

Paulist Press
New York/Mahwah, N.J.

Grateful acknowledgment is made for use of the following:
Prayers by Keith R. Crim, reprinted by permission of the editor, *The Presbyterian Outlook*, Richmond, Virginia. Prayers by Keith Crim from *The Upper Room Disciplines 1967*: Copyright © 1966 by The Upper Room. Used by permission of Upper Room Books. From *The Upper Room Disciplines 1972*: Copyright © 1971 by The Upper Room. Used by permission of Upper Room Books. Poems by Julia H. Crim originally printed in *The Lyric*: Used by permission of *The Lyric*. Material by Julia H. Crim that originally appeared in the *Journal of Christian Healing*: Used by permission of the *Journal of Christian Healing*, Association of Christian Therapists, 6728 Old McLean Village Drive, McLean, Virginia 22101. Poems and prayers previously published in Keith and Julia Crim, *Dying and Rising with Christ*, Abingdon Press: Used by permission of Abingdon Press. The authors would also like to thank Rev. Msgr. J. Kenneth Rush, Holy Cross Catholic Church, Lynchburg, Virginia, for his careful help in finding suitable scripture references from the *Lectionary for Mass*.

Cover design by William Campbell after Leonardo da Vinci

Library of Congress Cataloging-in-Publication Data

Crim, Julia H.
    Abound with blessings : a month of poems and prayers / Julia H. and Keith R. Crim.
    p. cm.
  Includes bibliographical references.
  ISBN 0-8091-3970-7 (alk. paper)
    1. Christian poetry, American. 2. Prayers. I. Crim, Keith R. II. Title.

  PS3553.R513 A64 2000
  811'.6—dc21

                                                              00-035616

Published by Paulist Press
997 Macarthur Boulevard
Mahwah, New Jersey 07430

www.paulistpress.com

Printed and bound in the
United States of America

Contents

For my husband
Keith Renn Crim
Who brings Christ to our world
Like lilies of the field springing up
Like mornings full of grace

ACKNOWLEDGMENTS

For their assistance and encouragement at the various stages of collecting the poems and prayers included in this volume, for their careful proofreading, and for their helpful suggestions, Keith and I wish to thank our daughter, Laura Renn Crim, a student at Davidson College, our dear friends Margaret Ward Morland, Poet Laureate of Virginia, and the Reverend John David Keister of Strasburg, Virginia, Robert G. Bratcher and Roger A. Bullard, translators with Keith for the American Bible Society, and H. McKennie Goodpasture, Professor Emeritus of Missiology, Union Theological Seminary in Virginia. We also are grateful for the cover drawing contributed by our son, William Campbell, and for the invaluable support and direction given us by our editor at Paulist Press, Donna Crilly. Above all, we thank Father Lawrence Boadt, CSP, Publisher of Paulist Press, for the opportunity to publish this book. As Keith's friend and colleague for thirty years, he has supported and encouraged us both from the beginning of this endeavor.

Foreword

Abound with Blessings is a remarkable collaboration between husband and wife, scholar and poet. Both, separately and together, have stood in the lion's den and walked through the valley of the shadow, and so are uniquely qualified as fellow pilgrims to walk this path with us.

Recognized for his brilliant biblical scholarship, the Rev. Dr. Keith Crim has contributed the daily prayers, their profound simplicity a perfect foil for the stunning variety of his wife's many-faceted poetry.

Julia Crim is a deeply committed Christian pastoral counselor and metaphysical poet. Her spiritual depth and reverence for the power of language are evident in her questions that have no quantifiable answers, and in her certain faith that God the Creator is her inspiration and the source of her poetry through which she catches glimpses of the unknowable Mystery that surrounds us and fills us with love and awe. In directing each poem to a specific biblical passage, she is sharing her personal experiences of faith and grace in the hope and belief that letting us listen to her heart in relation to scripture will bring our hearts closer to the understanding and peace we seek.

Words are her element. She swims in them, leaps like a colorful fish, floats, submerges, almost drowns, then rises on wings of the Word to thanksgiving and praise for the sensuous earth and the divine Spirit wherein she dwells, a celebration of our love of God and the world he made for us. The everyday becomes miraculous through her strangely pure imagination, linking Logos and Eros, reason and desire, in God's love for his people, Christ's love for his church.

The aural beauty of her poems may at times seem to veil the meaning, but we have only to step into the magic of her imagery to understand how the words mean more than they say—the essence of poetry. Julia Crim knows a poem is not the solution to a problem. A poem is music. Assonance and consonance, time, rhythm, and mood reinforce sound and feeling to etch our memory. The most intense lyricism infuses her poetry, so that we are released to explore our own feelings. Her lines are fluid, like a stream flowing toward the ocean, becoming one with the eternal Mystery. Our hearts beat with their rhythms, feel the sacredness of every encounter and join in the universal Song of Being.

The sacred expression of our spirit, the recurrent incantatory patterns, tell the poet a poem is prayer. It is offering to God all that we are and hope and believe, and asking for healing forgiveness and peace from the chaos of all we are not, our brokenness and separation.

A poem is love. Whatever the subject, love provides the creative energy, the nutrient in which the Spirit grows and fills the poem with truth and meaning. Then, love becomes the poem's dwelling place.

Lastly, a poem is miracle. After the fountain of inspired words has poured from the spring of the Spirit, it is only by grace—and hard work—that in the quiet stillness later, there stands the poem, fully formed and shining.

For its seekers, Julia and Keith Crim's work will prove to be much more than one month of poems and prayers. It will be an instruction, an inspiration, and an illumination for living *all days*. The waves of their words open the floodgates for us to examine our own life and faith, and we see our beggar's bowl filled to overflowing. We drink the sweet water, and find our fever cooled and our parched hearts healed. Drink deeply here, and be blessed.

—Margaret Ward Morland
Poet Laureate of the Commonwealth of Virginia

Introduction

This is a book of Christian poetry and prayer. This is also a book of pastoral care, for poetry is one of God's good gifts for healing. The apostle Paul, in 1 Corinthians 14:15, calls believers to pray and to sing with the Spirit and also with the understanding. The Christian poet is one who sings with the Spirit to bring understanding to the heart. The poet writes to gain inner wisdom and insight and to meet deep needs within. Creative tension comes first and then commitment to the working out of that tension by the giving of the self to its task. As Christians, when we experience inspiration in writing and reading, we yield ourselves to the power of the Spirit within that stands ready to lead us into all truth. In Romans 8:26 we have the promise that "The Spirit comes to help us, weak as we are. For we do not know how we ought to pray; the Spirit himself pleads with God for us in groans that words cannot express."

To sing with the Spirit by allowing the Holy Spirit to help us is an exhilarating and, at times, frightening experience, but it can bring insight and, above all, healing to all who open themselves to such an encounter. Kathleen Norris, in an article in *The Christian Century*, comments:

> ...a poem written because "I want to write a poem about Advent"—or about nuclear disarmament, for that matter, will usually be a dead poem. Good poems on those subjects can be written and are. But writing is something that is alive, beyond cognitive control.[1]

As Christians, we are "people of the Word." The power of the Word is the power, the beauty, and the mystery of the Lord himself. We transcend ourselves as writers and as readers when we are caught up in this power. Margaret Ward Morland describes this happening in a poem:

Transcendence

Who arabesque on air
Know this wisp of breath
Is not all.

Who tongue-touch a snowflake
Taste time as infinite
As hope.

Who find the universe
Within themselves envelop
Every one.

In love that makes
Them both more human
And divine.[2]

When we give ourselves permission to experience this ecstasy, we open ourselves to the possibility of healing. For it is in the very act of letting go that we find the everlasting arms of God upholding us. Then, in the process of creating, our subconscious and unconscious work in unity with the conscious mind. This allows the intellectual, volitional and emotional functions to act in harmony as Rollo May writes in *The Courage to Create*.[3]

> Just as healing comes to the poet in "the process of bringing something new into being,"[4] it may also come to the reader, for the emotion that poetry awakens within is the encounter between the image evoked by the poet and the same image sleeping within the reader.[5]

After the death of a patient with whom I had spent a good deal of time as a pastoral counselor, I wrote the following poem which helped me find healing and peace.

Feed My Lambs
John 21:15

It is in the letting go
That life is—
Beneath my apple tree
Petals fall away from
Leafing green.
I remember your voice
Falling away from me,

And your white, white hands
Lying
Pale as a dove's breast
Over mine.
Lady of tears,
You it was who questioned me
Concerning lambs.
Now,
Nestled in Light,
And nurtured there
Above the non-essential,
You are
Leafing green,
Petal free forever
From the night.[6]

"Like the parable and unlike the novel, the poem is episodic, usually concerned with a single life event or experience, with little or no attempt to explain how this event or experience fits within the larger life structure of the poet or the poet's subject."[7] The above poem tries only to speak truth about what was seen and felt in the face of certain loss. The German poet, Rainer Maria Rilke, encourages poets "to describe their sorrows and desires, passing thoughts, and the belief in some sort of beauty."[8] The Christian poet affirms that belief, that beauty is Christ. When we sing with the Spirit, our poems will speak truly about our sorrows, desires, thoughts, and beliefs, and will help heal us as we grow in understanding and peace.[9]

This book of poetry and prayer is divided into four sections, using the four verses of the prayer-poem, "Kyrie Eleison" as a guide. Addressing God first as Song Giver, the poems and prayers in Part 1 ask God for deliverance from our pain, guilt, and sorrow, and praise him for his mercy. The poems and prayers in Part 2 seek God as Hope Giver to still the anxiety of our minds, to increase our faith, and to help us to live with the mystery and uncertainty of life. In Part 3, the poems and prayers call out to God to be with us in the power of his eternal Word, and celebrate that in Christ all the promises of God find their Yes. In the final section, Part 4, the poems and prayers embrace God as Life Giver, praying that we may be made perfect in him and know that inexpressible joy of his presence and his peace.

Abound with Blessings seeks to respond from a Christian perspective to the deep spiritual longing that is increasingly manifest in recent American verse, a poetry that is in search of significance underneath and beyond the succession of temporal events.[10] Named from Old and New Testament passages, each of the poems in this book also includes references to scripture and companion prayers, reminding us that, as Christians, the significance underneath and beyond the succession of temporal events is Christ.

—*Julia Crim*

Notes

1. Kathleen Norris, "Finding a Place for Poets in the Church," *The Christian Century* (October 19, 1986), 1053–54.
2. Margaret Ward Morland, *It Happens Thus* (Lynchburg, Virginia: Bargara Press, 1983), 41.
3. Rollo May, *The Courage to Create* (New York: W. W. Norton & Co., 1975), 39.
4. Ibid.
5. Paul Tournier, *The Meaning of Persons* (New York: Harper & Row, 1957), 74.
6. Julia Campbell (Julia H. Crim), "Aldah," in *The Richmond Literature and History Quarterly* 1:3 (Winter 1978).
7. Donald Capps, *The Poet's Gift* (Louisville, Kentucky: Westminster/John Knox Press, 1993), 2.
8. Rainer Maria Rilke, *Letters to a Young Poet* (New York: W. W. Norton & Co., 1934), 19.
9. See also *Poetry the Healer*, edited by Jack J. Leedy (Philadelphia: J. B. Lippincott, 1973).
10. Denise Levertov, *New and Selected Essays* (New York: New Directions Books, 1992), 4.

Week One:
Songs and Prayers of Praise

SONG GIVER,
Deliver us from the atonal pain
That leaves us beyond
Our own heart's mercy.

SUNDAY 𝒮

Morning
With Wings As Eagles: An Invitation
Isaiah 40:31

These things
Are spoken of in themes
That merge the gentle and the swift.
I've heard that even eagles fly
Beyond the garden of desire,
And I believe that there may be
Remembered chasms of the mind
Where deer and antelope depart
From leafy groves of columbine
To tread the passages of sea
And listen to the dolphins sigh.
So come with me before the eve
Of all remarkable design,
And we will leap the chasm free,
And we will tread on mystery,
And we will hear the cherubim,
And comprehend,
And comprehend.

Prayer

God of wisdom, give us wisdom to know when and how to speak and when and how to be silent. Teach us to do Your holy will. Amen.

Evening
The Friend of God
James 2:23

Creative,
Innovative, clearing in my life—
Willing to risk the outstretched hand,
The open mind,
The abundant heart—
Seeking encounter,
While calling me into being,
Defining unity in a gesture,
Acceptance in a smile.
Your spirit is aglow
As the dawn uncovering green,
You are rich as a meadow,
Yielding as June,
Keeping always the personal harvest,

The cornucopia of care,
You are a bearer of grace,
A wounded healer cradling time
In the eternal now.

Prayer

*We praise You, Lord, for awakening our conscience in
our day. Continue to teach us what is good, and to send
prophets to work for justice in the world. Amen.*

MONDAY

Morning
Feed My Lambs
John 21:15

It is in the letting go
That life is—
Beneath my apple tree
Petals fall away from
Leafing green.
I remember your voice
Falling away from me,
And your white, white hands
Lying
Pale as a dove's breast
Over mine.
Lady of tears,
You it was who questioned me
Concerning lambs.
Now,
Nestled in Light,
And nurtured there
Above the non-essential,
You are
Leafing green,
Petal free forever
From the night.

Prayer

O Lamb of God, send us forth among this questing generation to be a redeeming power throughout Your great family on earth. Amen.

Evening
I Sing Praise unto Thee
Hebrews 2:12

Speak
And the mystery of all things made
Sings
Of the glory of Him who moves
Deep in the wells of human hearts,
Far in the realm of souls made new.
Heavenward!
Always, only this,
Christ at the head,
Our maker of joy,
Creator of words forever true,
Master of life
Unknowable, sure.

Shepherd of bliss,
Unsearchable, found.
Son of all silence,
Ineffable song.

Prayer
Help us, O Lord, to grow in our commitment to Your will so that by the things we say and the things we do we may praise You with faith, joy, and love. Amen.

TUESDAY 🙋

Morning
Like a Dove
Matthew 3:16

Before the Spirit like a dove descended,
The Spirit in the Word was One,
All heaven sang a new song praising Him,
And all Creation became His seamless throng.

By Every Word
Matthew 4:4

Whatever You give us
That much we are,
All wholeness as springtime
Moves through Your hand—
All growing Your giving
Restoring the heart,
All firstlings You've chosen,
For rhythms apart.

—9—

Spring forth now in glory
Most gentle, small Word,
Leap over our reigning,
Crumble our will,
Until we are gathered
All safe in Your grasp—
and dare to uncover
Our winters at last.

Prayer

You, O God, call us to a closer walk with You. Help us during our life's journey to grow in wisdom and clarity about the direction you want our lives to take, so that we may move straight toward the goal and be perfected in You. Amen.

Evening
There Was Given to Me
2 Corinthians 12:7

God of majestic love
Whose truth
Three times denied my passioned plea

For needs unmet, for rest, for ease,
And sealed eternally by grace
That rending of the thorn in flesh,
Forge me anew
That at the heart of my desire
I may be wholly yours—
Blest Holy Child of spirits free,
And Comforter sublime,
Thy will be done.

Prayer

O Lord, stretch our minds so that we may begin to understand who You are and have been from all eternity. Help us to understand the grace and dignity of Your knowledge and Your power. May we accept who we are and what You call us to be, strong because You have called us, and ready to do whatever You call us to do. Amen.

WEDNESDAY

Morning
In Green Pastures
Psalm 23:2

Concave vessel
Hemispherical
Or nearly so,
Larger than a cup
It runneth over—
I cannot hold it gently
For it spilleth over me,
Still
It holdeth many things—
Yea,
All things doth it hold
Save One
Whose pastures green I roam,
Whose valleys I have known.

A Little Child
Isaiah 11:6

Lion among dandelions,
You are today
Lord over green grasses growing,
King of loud roars.
Lion among dandelions,
Shout your world into spring,
Gather grace for your journey,
For you, child,
With nose and cheeks glistening pollen,
Are in green pastures
And leap beneath the sun,
While underneath
Are the Everlasting Arms.

Prayer
Almighty God, give us, we pray, the power and strength
of Your everlasting arms. Teach us to rely on You and
not on ourselves. Amen.

Evening
Behold My Hands
John 20:27

Before all stillness
I beheld you.
Beside the evening coming out of stars,
Before the sheltering of shadows,
When victory was an easy thing,
And grief an invention of the heart.
I beheld you becoming as the twilight
That traced your face in silhouette,
Your form caught in autumn colors
Of gold rushing before the wind,
Singing the falling of the night into mystery,
Searching meaning into movement,
Greeting and departing grace.
While all that you are
Gathered days like manna
Before the passage of pain.

Prayer
*You, Lord, lived as a man among us. You were tempted
in every way that we are, but You did not sin. Because
You understand how easily we are tempted, have mercy
on us. Help us to triumph over the sins that beset us so
easily. Amen.*

THURSDAY

Morning
Blessed Is He That Cometh
John 12:13

Tellers of tales and ancient bards,
Young prophets and sure shepherds,
Brothers and sisters in Christ,
"Sing with the Spirit,"
YES,
"And with the mind also."
Break the long silence
Of not being still,
Of not knowing—
GO!
"Swing wide the gates
That the King of Glory may come in"
And be welcomed at last!
NOW!
"As a still small voice,"
"As small rain,"
Whetting the ground of our souls
With desire for Him.
GREET!
With loud Hosannas His Spirit within,
While the Lord of Light

Passes on a young colt
The portals of our hearts.

Prayer

Help us, O Lord, to proclaim the good news of salvation now. We look forward to that day when there will be no more shyness about proclaiming Your name, no more uncertainty about who You are, no more turning from You in doubt and discouragement, no more self-glorification or blatant boasting. Then every one of Your creatures will call You Lord and give glory to God the Father. By Your saving work on the cross and Your rising from the tomb, we are saved. Even so, come, Lord Jesus. Amen.

Evening
The Voice of Weeping
Jeremiah 31:15

Caught in the spring
Of the mind's rush flowing
Away from the ache
Of one

Dissolved,
I yield
To the rain that brushes
Nothing that is—
All scarlet, all thorn
No fragrance
But the leaf wet earth,
No love,
But my own voice calling,
No rest,
But a falling away,
And still your voice
Touching me.

Prayer

God of the past, the present, and the future: The past is with us, sometimes as joy, sometimes as shame or sorrow. Our times are in Your hands. May our every day be lived to Your glory. Amen.

FRIDAY

Morning
For My Life Is Spent with Grief
Psalm 31:10

Before the dawn
I spread the essence green,
And dappled sun with grief
Where pastures lie.
I gathered berries
Ripe before the blue,
And fallen before autumn into dew.
Before the call of whippoorwill was heard,
I chose the apples far beyond my hills.
Before all goodness could be held and sealed
I left the fold
And wandered lost and proud
Until God brought me to my knees at last.
And there indeed I have my harvest found,
Though never beyond reason, only sight.
For I am dappled, fallen sure, and spilled,
And out of fold with self, and man, and God,
And see that I have always been in part,
But never known it in the silent heart.
At last with Job
In dust and ashes free,
I leap, I dance, I sing such mystery.

Prayer
Grant, most loving Lord, that we may joyfully surrender our lives to You and be ready to serve You and those You call us to serve. Amen.

Evening
A Remnant Shall Be Saved
Romans 9:27

Remarkable reason
I speak not,
Nor the unscheduled allure
Of all that glisters—
I know that gold comes
Surely through earthen vessels,
And nothing but the mystery remains
As the body is broken,
As the vessel spills its wine
Into the open hand of memory.
There is,
In the coming together of our hearts,
Much that does not meet—
Bridges are broken,

Roads are swamped,
Paths uprooted,
But the Eternal Word remains for each
The saving remnant.

Prayer

From the lowest depths, our Lord and Savior, You were raised to the highest place of all, higher than the blessed powers that do Your holy will. Lift our eyes above to behold Your glory and to take fresh courage from Your victory. Make our hearts brave again and our arms strong. Amen.

SATURDAY

Morning
Seek Ye First the Kingdom of God
Matthew 6:33

How dare a heart such blessedness receive,
How trust a self entrusted with such love?
Such depths I plunge only to believe
Your words are green and will all seasons prove—
All melody is ours, all rustling leaves
That dance the autumn air, all midnight stars
Reclaiming earth to blossom winter trees,
All light years leaped disarming temporal bars,
All, all are ours as we are His alone.
So dare I trust to yield and yielding be
Found free to hear hosannas ring,
found whole to sense eternity.
My love, upon clay feet I risen stand
Beside you earthside of that mansioned land.

Prayer
*O Lord of all the ages, free us to recognize the real riches
of our inheritance from the past and to be loyal to it in a
way that will enrich the present and the future, for us
and for all your people. Amen.*

Evening
With the Spirit
1 Corinthians 14:15

Without the muse,
In faith I sing,
Bereft of innocence within,
I keep the loss of days and nights
For petals I have seen in flight.
I know the taste of Living Bread,
And see its leaven lift in you,
And hear the question of your heart
Reach out for all that bread renews.
So speak, and gently will He come,
Or call, and let Him gather you
Around His table glad and free.
Be not afraid to beggar be—
I am a beggar, can't you see?

Of the Crumbs Which Fall
Matthew 15:27

"God inviting God beyond God's limits"
Lifts me up,
Gives fleeting song to measured grace,
Restores peripheral blessing,
Moderates goodness into order,
And allows the beating heart
To leap the limits that would bind it,
To the freedom that is Christ.

Prayer
O God, help us always to look forward to the goal of the race which we have entered. In remembrance of You, help us to be loyal to the unknown future. Amen.

Week Two:
Songs and Prayers of Hope

HOPE GIVER,
Make still the unease of our minds
With the glad certainty
That all mystery is understood in You.

SUNDAY 🌰

Morning
A Live Coal in His Hand
Isaiah 6:6

Burning bright,
Fire of God,
Cleansing infirmity
In the basin of pain,
Touch our hearts today
With living coals
That we may turn and be healed,
And praise.

Prayer
God of Mercy, open our eyes to Your word and to our world. There is work to do in the world around us. Justice is denied, resources are squandered, and lives are destroyed. Help us to attend to what You say through the scripture and respond. Amen.

Evening
Caught Up into Paradise
2 Corinthians 12:3

Caught—
Beyond, before, under, above—
Caught up in Truth,
Tremulous before experience
Confirms ecstasy,
And reflects the face translucent
Beyond cause to Causer.
Finite we speak with the mind
Beginning words—
Infinite, the Word speaks through us
Wisdom and grace,
To greet the other in the self
And God in all—
Listen, the wind listeth,
The lilac blooms again.

Prayer

O God, we thank You that even though we cannot now fully understand what You are doing through us or through Your church, we can still move forward in faith, trusting our lives and our security to You, as we can also rejoice in the riskiness of being a Christian. Amen.

Morning
With Great Joy
Luke 24:52

Song of songs
Our hearts are beating,
Joy unfolding, living, breathing.
Trusting Him, we found His good,
Risking faith, we understood.
  There was a time
  A life ago,
  Our hearts were stone
  Afraid to grow,
  Afraid to let another in,
  Afraid to cast ourselves
  On Him—
  Afraid of days,
  Afraid of being,
  'Til Love caught us
  and gave life meaning.
  That day we turned
  And found Him there
  To meet our trust,
  To bear our care,
  And saw His love

Was everywhere!
Shining out of children's eyes
Hung in stars across the skies,
Blossoming in early spring
Lifted high on feathered wings,
Above the peaks, beneath the seas
Whispering through mighty trees,
In lunar space behind the moon
Within the walls of every room,
Waiting, hoping
Knocking, reaching
Renewing hearts,
Touching, healing.
Dawn of dawns
We greet you singing,
Joy unfolding, giving, being
Finding Him, ourselves are found,
Yielding death, in Life abound.

Prayer

Lord, give us a sense of expectancy as we face the mystery of Your will. Help us to yield our lives in obedience to You and experience Your love upholding us. Amen.

Evening
My Soul in Drought
Isaiah 58:11

Swung from the rim
Of an Amazon drought
I drift through the wind
Of an unfinished growing,
Till freed by your eyes
Near the haunt of the owl,
I am gathered in down
Of milkweed pod, knowing
A meadow I have never known
In the tremor of your lips.
"The threshold is the thing," you say,
"In art, in music, rhythm, form,
God is love upon the brink."
And then, as though too much were said
For afternoon conjecture,
You fold your hands and turn away
From Renoir, God, and meadows.
Still, I have felt a unicorn
Move across your heart,
And nourished by such tapestry.
Flourishing depart.

Prayer

O Lord, beyond everything we can know as Christians lies Your mystery. Beyond the boundaries of our experiences is a vast, unfathomed world of Your truth. But You sent Your Son into the world to reveal to us Your love and Your forgiveness, and in Him we see You and find peace. Amen.

TUESDAY

Morning
Near Damascus
Acts 9:3

Whatever reason cannot be,
Forever aching memory
That casts the line in foreign seas
To gather emptiness from dreams.
It is not what we name as need,
Or want, or thorn that pierces,
Bleeds, and scorns all effort to allay.
Instead it is a road, a path,
A radiance in the mind at last
That leads us past our recklessness
And heals us from all harms,
A quiet grove, a still repose
And grace once more to see.

Prayer
Lord, we know that You are calling us through Christ to be Your servants in the world. Give us the joy of recognizing who You are and the confidence of serving You daily. Amen.

Evening
He Went Away Sorrowful
Matthew 19:22

When I was first encompassed by Your eyes,
I knew.
Long before Your words traced silver sketches
In my mind,
Or colored the beats of my heart
With alternating grays and greens,
I knew.
I felt Your tides sweep across my inner bay,
Watched the texture of Your skin yielding
To the downward plunge of wave,
And heard Your call rise from my depths
And shine across Your waiting, salty face.
While I,
Tossed like foam along the shore of knowing
And desiring all Your flow,
Turned from Your face,
And fled away.

Prayer
Jesus is the Messiah! Thank you, Lord, that we no longer need to puzzle over Your identity, or to wonder why You spoke and acted as You did, but may choose to follow You joyfully. Amen.

WEDNESDAY

Morning
I Know That My Redeemer Liveth
Job 19:25

Everlasting Lord,
Preserver of our hearts and of our heartbeats,
Protect us TODAY in the shadow of Your wings,
Hide us TODAY in the peace of Your Spirit,
Help us TODAY to walk upon Holy Ground,
Lift us TODAY in Your everlasting arms,
Gentle our fears TODAY in the hollow of Your hand,
And seal us FOREVER in Your eternal love,
That we may turn to YOU and be healed.

Prayer
God of mercy, by your grace today we have seen the world in a new light, and we have seen what You expect of us. Call us into Your service in Your church triumphant. Amen.

Evening
Except Thou Bless Me
Genesis 32:26

Before what is
Must always be
Becoming joy,
Unleashed by grief.
Before each name
We cannot choose
Waits wisdom
To be called by God.
Upon your face
That call I see,
Reflected there
I see His light.
You see it not,
Nor can you see
What lives within
And shines without.
But others see
And know that you
Have pilgrimage made
To Peniel,
And there alone
Have wrestled long,
And blessing won,
And blessing won.

Prayer

O Lord, we know that only what we do for You is permanent. You call us in Christ to serve in ways we cannot predict in advance. They may not be the ways we choose; they may even seem insignificant. But Lord, may we always remember that only You bless, that only from You do we receive recognition that does not fade. Amen.

THURSDAY ✍

Morning
The Voice of My Beloved
Song of Solomon 2:8

Your song
Pure luster caught in flame,
Remembered radiance spilling forth,
Your eyes embellish me with joy.
I will leap up and risk the pain,
I will lie down and bear the thought
That no wings lift away the night.
But come
And now unfold my spring,
Down petaled ways I see the rain,
Still come and gather in my eyes,
And sing me over with your hands.
I want to listen to your face,
And taste your very words tonight.

Prayer
Lord Christ, how much we need the sense of awe that causes us to sink to our knees and exclaim, "You are the Messiah!" Thank You for giving us the warmth of Your

fellowship as we respond to Your call and as we walk with You day by day. Amen.

Evening
A Friend Loveth
Proverbs 17:17

Claim all the gold,
The accent of this early morn
Repeats the fragrance of the early year,
And all about
The rhythm of the air
Is sweet with apples falling to the earth.
I cannot give you answer for the years,
Or yet the answer for each hour we shared—
We spoke, we paused, we trembled in alarm
Between the outstretched hand and ample fruit.
So harvest is,
So always has it been—
The coming clean,
The gathering of bounty in each barn,
The gathering of gold in every heart.

Lest all be lost, we bind what we have known
Within a form definable by touch as well as mind,
That in the pure cold of wintering
The pure gold of meaning will remain.

Prayer

Lord, plant our feet on the rock. Place in our hands the key to freedom from bondage and sin. Help us to unlock the fetters of fear and confess You before others in the freedom You give us. Amen.

FRIDAY 🎵

Morning
As a Tree Planted
Psalm 1:3

In the early days
Near memory beginning,
There was a white-locked man
Whose eyes held autumn blue
As merrily at the end
As when one child
Unchiseled by the years
First followed him
Past fields of buds unfolding,
Up hills of grasses whispering by knees,
Into the silent meadows of the heart,
Where grew the Tulip Tree.
The dawn revealed
Diffuses us with light,
Slowly and gently at the start,
But stronger when the eyes begin to see.
The morning lingers
In the webs of night,
The longbow of the sun
Quivers over fiddleheads of ferns,
And feathers,
Cleaving catkin

—41—

Thrust suddenly into wind,
From out the Tulip Tree.
Upon this earthen wheel we turn,
Against the wind our clay—
All form emerges
As it has to be.
Along the pilgrim way we cannot know
Lie peaks, like dreaming maidens, all
Concealed,
Appearing, as the moon breaks through the clouds,
Full-breasted offerings
They silent stand.
'Til silvered by the touch of rising stars
Moving softly over shadowed limbs,
Green tresses fall
Beneath the Tulip Tree.
Oh winged light,
Descending is your flight,
Through tulip bloom
The howling night.
Before the broken shells
And naked song you longed to hear
I watch you weave.
Beneath the Tulip Tree I stand
Where all is of another hue,
And nothing green,
And weave with you—
Still greens the Tulip Tree.
Oh Tulip Tree of tulip bloom,
Everywhere flowering,

Everywhere scattering—
Over ferns leafing,
Over first violets gathering
Your orange-gold dust of life,
How many nestlings have you sheltered
As you sheltered me!
How many crickets
Sounded their first songs
Against your sturdiness
And heard being echo,
Or mosses,
Shielded by your broad expansiveness,
Catapulted their joy into spring.
Oh Tulip Tree,
Into the open mouth of emptiness
All milk tooth days unfold at last.
Oh Tulip Tree,
My white-locked Tulip Tree!
The seasons pass more hastily than hours,
Where grief winds up to meet the night,
Green words, unharvested,
Lie scattered with the flowers.
But love,
Remembering you
With fields of buds unfolding,
Up hills of grasses whispering by knees,
At last I see
How held your eyes the autumn blue,
And with a joy more ponderous than pain
The silent meadows of my heart renew.

Prayer

O Lord, our Lord, help us to live as trees planted by living water, empowered in this world for the good of Your people. Help us to remember that Your church is built on a living foundation of faith. Amen.

Evening
With My Own Hand
1 Corinthians 16:21

Here I will write you a letter,
Still as the moment of grace,
Here I will gather the pages
That fell in another place.
Now is the moment of meeting,
Hushed is the opening space,
Where poet, prophet, and teacher
Tremble their lives to trace,
Seek for the wisdom to follow
Crumbs fallen and scattered before,
A path that lies sheltered in longing
Near the Presence that walks before.

Prayer

Lord, we thank You, that as we read Your word and open our hearts to You, You give us the same assurance You gave the apostles. Help us to make Your word a part of our daily lives. Amen.

SATURDAY 🖋

Morning
Children Are a Heritage
Psalm 127:3

"O come, let us sing to the Lord"
A song of thanksgiving and praise
For our children—
For their birth,
For the pain of their coming,
For the joy of their being.
Bone of our bone, and
Flesh of our flesh—
For this and more
"Now thank we all our God,"
For those we have borne,
For those we have cared for and taught,
And for all we have loved
We say,
"How abundant is your goodness,"
For our children have taught us our own need,
Helped us to grow, helped us to change,
Helped us to become more what You, Lord,
Would have us be for them and for You.
O Lord, we lift up our souls to You
And give thanks even for the hard moments,

The painful hours, and anxious days with our children—
For we found and are finding the courage to let go
And give our children the freedom to be Your own.
We thank You for their struggles,
And for our own hearts yearning for them,
And for their lives.
For all of our hopes, prayers, joys, and tears
For our children
We give You praise and thanks.

Prayer

Thank you, Lord, that the promise You gave to Peter was a liberating promise. It gave to the apostle and to the church the freedom and the power to be God's instruments in the world. As parents and teachers, and friends, "Freedom is what we have—Christ has set us free" (Gal 5:1 TEV). Amen.

Evening
Honor Thy Father
Exodus 20:12

Spring eternal, golden girl,
Spring up, like lilies of the field,

Rise up, like mornings full of grace.
Spring eternal, golden girl,
Like lilies of the field—
Thrice blessed, your lashes greet me,
Unsettled silk surrounds you,
Smooth as your cheek is rose.
Your father, my love,
Is like a red, red rose,
Like you, he is the morning sun,
Light changing dew into diamonds
In every web of night,
Faith changing water into wine,
He gently leads us both.
Music he is to us,
Still as the evening prayer
He sings to you—
Your hands in his,
Perfectly matched prayer beads.
He brings
Christ to our world
Like lilies of the field
Springing up,
Like mornings full of grace.

Prayer

Lord, help us never to forget that Your summons leads to Your glory. Whether You call us as individuals or call us as Your church, the goal of that call is to reveal Your greatness and to lead us to praise You through our lives. Amen.

Week Three:
Songs and Prayers of Grace

GRACE GIVER,
Come swiftly to us
With the power of Your eternal Word
Which is always yes to all who seek You.

SUNDAY

Morning
Come unto Me
Matthew 11:28

If I speak in the rhythm of the broken lute,
If I sing in the melody of fallen rain,
Will you hear my voice still?
The invitation is out.
Unstructured by the cell,
It is surreal as heavy mist,
Needing distance to be found in.
And always time is hard,
Like the coming to greet oneself.
For if these frail vessels hold gold enough
It is to regard the stars themselves with green—
If not, the robe unravels fire.
Seeing what I am alone,
I sing for Him who took me unrehearsed
And called me "thou,"
That I might speak no more in mystery,
But release my atoms to the earth,
Find peace in shadows ceasing.

Prayer
O Lord, we pray for the grace to let the light of Your love shine through us so that those who see us will praise You. Amen.

Evening
The Light of the World
John 8:12

Gather and scatter,
Garner and waste,
But only one Light
Through the valley of shadows,
Only one Love
No darkness confounds.

Prayer
O Lord, we love You now and for all time. Help us in all our work for You to be true. Help us to love Your people and bring them the good news of Your salvation. Amen.

MONDAY

Morning
Many Waters Cannot Quench Love
Song of Solomon 8:7

Song-bearer, depart,
Weave not your garland now,
Nor tell of gardens costly and perfumed.
I am not ready to sing the bartered note,
Nor join the throng of souls beyond reproach.
Escape into our room is all I ask
Before the evening hour.
Don't leave me still apart
From that rich place. I know
The contour of your mouth too well—
That dear, uneven line I love to trace
When all the sweetness of your face I hold.

Prayer
Father, we know that You hear us in our pain. We open our hearts to You and long for You to bless us. We ask You to give us wholeness and maturity as individuals. Teach us to praise You with our lives. Amen.

Behold the One
Eternal Gift,
Our Lord and Savior
In your thoughts
For widow, orphan,
All the weak
Whose need is great,
Whose power is small.

You are a friend
God sends to these
To guide, establish, and protect.
With ready grace
And steady smile
You calm the faltering
With His peace.

You are the friend
God sent to us
In time of endless trial and pain
To help with burdens,
Clear our paths,

And hostel us within your Inn
Of charity made care.
God grant us never to forget
Remembrance for the things that were
So long ago,
Now lost and still
But safe with God till all is well
And in the Kingdom
We might thank God for you still.

Prayer

Let us praise God for those who have helped us through difficult days, so that the world may praise God for sending His good Samaritans into the world. Amen.

TUESDAY ✌

Morning
I AM THAT I AM
Exodus 3:14

I am a God
That is neither yes nor no,
But Alpha and Omega—all.
Far away beyond distant stars
Is the "Sibling of our spirits,"
Evoker of our souls,
Listener to our questions.
Far away in our inmost being
Where we know we stand on holy ground
Is the God who stands with us.
A voice cries in the wilderness,
"Child, you are
Image of my Image,
Soul of my Soul."
I AM calls you forth
To redemption of the withered life,
To the joy of resistance fled,
To the clarity of mystery embraced.

Prayer

O God, we are made in Your image. Help us to use our strength to remove the injustices of society. Call us forth to build more perfect institutions, so that Your glory may be known throughout the world. Amen.

Evening
A Far Country
Luke 15:13

Boxes of books everywhere,
Pictures unhung and scattered
Frame these fragment rooms.
Light streams through dirty windows
Into the apartment I am leaving.
Once every shred was whole,
Smooth as your skin.
I would gather you up and carry you
From room to room to see
Sun sparkled each window.
In daylight, your fingers found my breasts,
At night I searched your fragrance.
When your birth curls fell, I thought,

This is the first of many partings.
How truth etches itself into subtle longing.
Finally your eyes relinquished mine.
Your face was empty as these rooms are now,
And I felt framed and scattered.
That is why I have given up this lease,
I have no elder son, no fatted calf—
You only were.

Prayer

O Lord, help us to yield our lives in obedience to You and to experience Your forgiveness. Take charge of our lives and show us that You are in charge of all and teach us, Lord, to hope all things. Amen.

WEDNESDAY

Morning
Some Seeds Fell
Matthew 13:8

There is,
In the falling of petals,
An April sound of leaving that is not uncertain,
Not cruel—no chill in their falling,
No final hope.
I have not found it so in lives falling.
Some fall with grace, it is true,
Though there is still the awe,
The uncertainty—the eyes like stars
Distant and cold falling into oblivion,
Or filled with tears, trembling
On the brink of letting go,
Before the passing of the night.
And is it too much,
The green-golden spun fields of spring,
The breath of nature rich with life,
All, all beneath this blue brilliance
Where morning stars sing the form of silence in
At our season's end?
Then, past all that is golden or wreathed in rose
We are caught in the eternal moment, near death,

Where senses are flooded,
And harmony is sought within and without.
Then patient, family, and givers of care
Become the circle where the Holy One is found.

Prayer
O God, in the midst of all our work, give us Your grace.
Let us always remember to ask if what we do brings
glory to You, for only what we do for You will last.
Amen.

Evening
Into His Chambers
Song of Solomon 1:4

In the room of my words
I will welcome you,
With the tongue of my song
I will cover you.
My vowels will all be joyful,
Consonants of us
Will melt along the currents of my skin,

Up and down the electric flow
Of loving you,
Of loving You!

Prayer

O God, we thank You that in this life, You have made us male and female and called it good. Help us to be grateful husbands and wives. Amen.

THURSDAY

Morning
There Was Born a Son
1 Samuel 1:20

Birth curls falling
Under the steady cut
Of a stranger's hand,
Babyhood melting before
My misty eyes as
Little boy face emerges.
Pleasure and pain united
In one moment
Of exquisite sweetness,
In this place, today,
Where has begun
The first of many partings.

Prayer
O Lord, help us to make our homes and families havens of love and understanding, and let us seek to strengthen all families. Work through us, that Your glory may be known. Amen.

Evening
The Good Treasure
Luke 6:45

> Carrying clover,
> In small hands clasped tight,
> The white blooms, a treasure
> Lifted to light,
> Are borne on the run
> With tip-toeing pleasure,
> And given to one
> Who did not remember
> That clover's a treasure.

Prayer

O God, beyond everything we can know lies the mystery of You. Beyond the boundaries of our experiences is the vast, unfathomed world of Your truth. Give us a sense of expectancy as we face the mystery of Your will. Amen.

FRIDAY ✍

Morning
They Were Sore Afraid
Luke 2:9

There was
A star last night,
A brighter, larger star than I had seen before,
A gleaming beacon, full and flashing forth,
The glorious message of a glorious birth.
O, prophets how your prophesies have bloomed,
But shepherds old, and worn and frail as I,
Have waited long and known such grief in life,
Our hearts all tremble to accept the Truth.
Make no mistake, we want to come to You,
To open wide our lives, to let You in,
We only ask for trust to dare the way,
That we may find new hope on manger hay.

Prayer
O God, we thank You that as Christians we find Your mystery, awesome as it is, does not frighten or disturb us because You are behind that mystery and have sent Your Son into the world to reveal Your love and Your forgiveness to us all. Amen.

Evening
In Remembrance of Me
Luke 22:19

Beloved Maitre d'
Plentiful feast,
Prepared beatitude
Of Providence spent—
Rapture recounted
In service restored,
Remembered in fullness,
Washing our feet—
Loaves beside fishes,
Beloved by friends,
Gathered to golden,
Passover feast—
Guests of His Presence,
Banquet of grief,
Harvest of hunger,
Replete in His Word.

Prayer
Father, by our Lord's example help us to serve our fellow Christians so that Your church may be carried across all barriers, revealing Your greatness and calling all to remembrance and praise. Amen.

SATURDAY

Morning
New Creation
Galatians 6:15

And the New Year comes,
Swiftly as ever and too soon
For all the losses to be borne
For all the past gladness to be remembered.
We feel too late,
In the silver hush,
Waiting for the star's gift,
Wondering how the coming days will
Bring us bearing gifts to the manger once again
Knowing no gold, no frankincense, no myrrh matters,
But only the gift of ourselves.
That only, as we are clay in the Potter's hands,
Can the Child we search for find us
In this New Year
And make of us His New Creation.

Prayer
*O Lord, our loving Father, help us in all that You call us
to do to be Your people, and keep us in Your joy as we*

labor for You. Be with all those who serve You in every place, and keep us all in Your grace. Amen.

Evening
The Veil of the Temple
Mark 15:38

Heavy fullness
Yielding to
And fast becoming pain—
Unbearable yet borne
Until the grand release—
Like tears that leap
The bounds of lash,
The milk came down,
Came down at last.
And more than that I have to tell—
But wait and catch the melody
Of starlight tasting beads of night.
For I was present when He died,
I felt the temple veil unwind
And rend the labyrinth of mind,
I saw the minotaur at last

Enveloped in a burning cask,
And found the place where swallows fly,
Within a vesseled being, I.
The whither of the blowing wind
Was seen at last as opening.
And in that golden breath of air
I knelt and bathed myself in myrrh,
Then rose before a candle lit
And robed myself in frankincense.

Prayer

O Lord, let us work and pray for peace among the nations of the world so that the nations may glorify the God of peace and reveal His greatness. Amen.

Week Four:
Songs and Prayers of Life

LIFE GIVER,
Wipe away our tears
And lead us into Your new creation
Triumphant in Christ.

SUNDAY ✍

Morning
In the Beginning
John 1:1

I am enveloped
In strokes of speaking rhythms,
Sounds surge in the underbreath.
The Word beneath the word
Is the word I feel.
I do not soar on syllables of clay,
But sing for the lily of the field
That blooms beneath my tongue—
His fragrance glides
Through all my body spaces.

Prayer

Almighty God, we thank You that You are present with us to give us strength, to bless us and to help us. We pray for those who grieve, those who are struggling with painful losses, those who need our help, those who weep over the evil in the world and the suffering that is there. May we also reach out to one another in love, in comfort, in sharing the strength that Christ gives us, that through Him we may be made more than conquerors

because He loved us, and gave Himself for us, and
promised us the gift of eternal life in His presence. To
Him be the glory and the power forevermore. Amen.

Evening
My Grace Is Sufficient
2 Corinthians 12:9

God of all grace
That gathers dawn
And nestles eventide
In peace,
Preserve
Our coming forth to sing
Our praise to You in everything—
Arms brushed by thorn
To fragrance bear,
Face caught in storm
Till wet with care,
And all the stars,
Like burning coals,
Cast by Your hand
To cleanse our souls.

For these and all You do
We sing,
Dark nights, long days,
Each pilgrimage.

Prayer

O God, we thank You that through Christ we become Your children and are able to set out for the goals You set for us, the way Abraham set out for an unknown land. On our journeys of faith, we are guided by the record of what You have done for Your people through all the centuries and the record of what You taught them through Your prophets and preachers. Amen.

Morning
Behold a Virgin

Behold a virgin
Bearing Truth
To us on Christmas morn;
Beyond eternity
Her rose
The stem of Jesse born
Enfolded bud
Of wondrous bloom
Glad angels first proclaim.
Such bliss poor shepherds early find
In swaddling clothes God's Light to all.
God's Grace to all mankind.
   Now will you come, beloved friends
   His Yuletide feast to share.
   Come singing, dancing, weeping,
   praising,
   Emmanuel declare.

Prayer
Dear Lord, our loyalty to You includes a fidelity to Your ongoing purpose in the years ahead. The example and

testimony of those who served You in the past stimulate us to make a contribution now that will bring blessing later on. We have Your promise, Lord, to be with us as we seek to live for You. Amen.

Evening
In the Same Country Shepherds
Luke 2:8

They brushed aside the thistles with their feet,
And tousled fallen leaves before their way.
Bearing the wind, they braced the frost to reap
One cord of wood, and gathered more that day
Than they would need to burn against the night;
Then pulled it home through tangle and through vine
And stacked it all together to the right
Of their back path, beside the sheltering pine.
That day they were a team, those harvesters
Of many fallen limbs, they shared the cold
To find the warmth they sought and bore it home.
More had each gathered than a hearth's reserve,
More had each heart confirmed than could be told—
Something they hoped was there, but had not known.

Prayer

Father, You have called us to do Your work. We come with a sense of weakness and inadequacy. We see how big the job is that You have given us, and we know that by ourselves we do not have the strength to do it. Aroused by the vision of what the world could be, help us to be faithful to the work You have called us to do. Amen.

TUESDAY

Morning
Be Still and Know
Psalm 46:10

And are we still?
Grand Voice, for You we yearn—
Storm fury over sand,
Wasteland of straw hope
We come, with Jeremiah, to know
The heart is deceitful above all things,
And utterly corrupt;
Who can understand it?
Still we come,
Yearning for Your eternal grasping,
Ecstasy
    of heart,
        soul,
            and mind,
                all in Your hand.
We cry aloud for a word,
        a sign,
            a vision,
While now, as then,
Your still small voice
Gathers us beneath
The wings of grace.

Prayer

O God, we thank You that Your church transcends barriers of nation, language, and race. We pray that we will be loyal to the fellowship of God's people, and that, as we seek to understand those unlike ourselves, we will let our thought patterns be brought more into conformity with the mind of Christ. Amen.

Evening
Serve the Lord
Joshua 24:15

Serving Him
Bestows peace.
Beyond redemption,
Eternity lifts the face to God,
Remakes the will,
Embellishes living
With humility,
Brings gifts to the King
Wrapped in tears of repentance,
Glistening white,
Purified by His grace,
Impeccable as His justice.

Prayer

Almighty God, we thank You that our loyalty to You calls us to be loyal to Your people. Help us to remember that there is no loyalty without profound personal involvement. Help us, in addition to our talents, to give also to those we serve the warmth of understanding that comes as we share both our minds and our hearts.
Amen.

Morning
As a Lamp That Burneth
Isaiah 62:1

The page was folded,
Still and white,
Before the passing of the night.
I kept the hope, the promise gone,
Eternity was all my loss
Sealed in an amber air—
Until you opened years of grief
With living words of care.
Again God's grace
Brought us to share,
In mutual space to pray—
To lift those clear and silent hymns,
Such essence now remembered brings
Love's presence and Love's peace.
As in creation, it is good
That leads the heart in quiet trust
To share the covenant of hope
Beside another's pain.
Thus, you have been my guardians
Along remembered days of old
That were both sad and good,

Both sad and good.
And you have been my listeners
Before the silence of the dawn.
You've kept the golden hearth in warmth,
The lamp is lit,
The feast prepared,
And I am ready to let go.

Prayer

Our Father, help us to seek reconciliation whenever needed with our fellow Christians. Remind us that we are forgiven only as we forgive others, and help us to be willing to let our hearts be softened by the fellowship of other Christians within the church. Amen.

Evening
Our Lord and Our God
John 20:28

Your Holy Week is upon us,
Your passion is a wreath around us—
The circle of Your overcoming love.
In the light of your giving,
We lie exposed.

Created in Your image,
All that is clay within us cries out with HOPE
That our wills,
Like wanton prodigals
Still in the far country,
May turn to you and be healed.
Created in Your image,
All that is clay within us cries out for MERCY,
For we are a mystery to ourselves
And to each other.
We claim you as Lord of life
And embrace death,
We are ashamed to stand by You
Even in our everyday encounters,
And before Calvary we flee You,
Ourselves, and each other.
Created in Your image,
All that is clay within us cries out for WISDOM
To hear Your call to the abundant life
And the grace to respond.
Lord have mercy upon us,
Grant us Your HOPE,
Christ have mercy upon us,
Teach us Your WISDOM.
Give us the grace
To learn as little children
That even these hardened hearts of ours
May be changed,
that we may rise with You
And call You blessed.

Prayer

O God, sometimes we hold back, knowing that it hurts to get involved. When we open our hearts, we face the possibility of being wounded by the wounds inflicted on others. That is what happened to the One by Whose wounds we are healed, the One Who calls us to follow Him. Amen.

THURSDAY 🐟

Morning
Abound with Blessings
Proverbs 28:10

Child—   Go in the knowledge
             That you are loved.
             Love in the knowledge
             That God loves you.
             Yours is the world
             As you are God's.
God is before all worlds unseen.
             Seen in the regions
             That faith makes free,
             Heard in the music
             That hope makes sure,
             Felt in the presence
             That love makes good.
Go with our blessing,
Bless and be blessed.

Prayer
O God, help us to place our faithfulness completely in You. Help us to put You at the center of our lives, so that all other loyalties to church, family, work, and

friends will be properly related to our first loyalty to You. Amen.

Evening
In the Dance
Psalm 149:3

Beloved, you will fly with wings
Like silver dust in downy cloud,
Your beating heart will lift you up
Above the toes you dance upon.
Your spirit in your dance will shine,
And dancer for the Lord, you'll be,
For He, the Lord of all the dance
Sees all your hope and He will lead.

Prayer
O God, help us to remember that loyalty to family is best attained by devotion to You. Teach us that even the dearest human relationships must not be put ahead of our faithfulness to You, and that as our family relationships take on their proper character, our fellowship with You will be renewed. Amen.

Friday ❧

Morning
Trust in the Lord
Psalm 37:3

O little one that I have borne,
I look into your morning face,
So new, so fresh, so all untried,
And recognize your separate place.
And pray that you will early choose
To trust your will to God,
And in the wholeness of His peace,
In His love abide.

Prayer
O Lord, we thank You that our allegiance to You helps us find where our loyalties should lie. Because we have You, Lord, we have the hope of unity that Your Spirit gives. We pray that You will make us instruments of reconciliation. Amen.

Evening
A Wise Man
Matthew 7:24

Tall of heart and stature,
Gentle as a child,
Full of wisdom greeting grace
At the foot of the mountain,
For there is always the Rock behind you,
The sturdy presence of faith
Moving with face uplifted
Through so many storms and losses—
So many triumphs too!
Laureate of goodness making peace
With bond and free,
You call us to stand tall with you
In this land of liberty.

Prayer
*O God, You have taught us that we cannot really be
loyal to our duty to Your people if we do not share with
them the highest good in life, loyalty to You. Help us to
point those we serve beyond ourselves to Christ, that at
the foot of the cross we may all be one in Him. Amen.*

SATURDAY 🌾

Morning
We Shall Be Like Him
1 John 3:2

Loving Him
Is movement beyond form
Into essence.
It is freedom wholly bound
To grace falling upon holy ground.
His presence
Sighs down the slope of morning prayer,
Enters the gospel of our skins
And makes us shining testaments of Him.

Prayer
Almighty God, we thank You for the challenge of believing in You and of following You day by day. Give us faithfulness in our lives. Give us creativity in our imaginations and in our ability to think beyond the obvious and to discover new truths, new power in the world, and to discover anew and in a rich way Your presence with us and Your blessing upon us. For we pray in Christ's name. Amen.

Evening
Kyrie Eleison
Psalm 30:10

SONG GIVER
Deliver us from the atonal pain
That leaves us beyond
Our own heart's mercy.

HOPE GIVER
Make still the unease of our minds
With the glad certainty
That all mystery is understood in You.

GRACE GIVER
Come swiftly to us
With the power of Your eternal Word
Which is always YES to all who seek You.

LIFE GIVER
Perfect us in Your peace
And lead us into your new creation
Triumphant in Christ.

Prayer

Almighty God, Your prophet Jeremiah earned the right to denounce evil because he felt compassion for all those who had done wrong. Help us to follow Jeremiah's example and attack the wrongs being done around us. Give us compassion for those who do wrong, who exploit the poor, who lie to the helpless, and who cheat minorities. Help us to keep Your call always before us as we give You praise. Amen.